SPEAKING SKILLS FOR TEENS

Create the Image You Desire

a 14-Session Speaking Seminar

PARTICIPANT MANUAL

BY GAIL A. CASSIDY

SPEAKING SKILLS FOR TEENS

Create the Image You Desire

a 14-Session Speaking Seminar

PARTICIPANT MANUAL

BY GAIL A. CASSIDY

BALBOA.PRESS

A DIVISION OF HAY HOUSE

Balboa Press books may be ordered through booksellers or by contacting:

Balboa Press
A Division of Hay House
1663 Liberty Drive
Bloomington, IN 47403
www.balboapress.com
1 (877) 407-4847

Because of the dynamic nature of the Internet, any web addresses or links contained in this book may have changed since publication and may no longer be valid. The views expressed in this work are solely those of the author and do not necessarily reflect the views of the publisher, and the publisher hereby disclaims any responsibility for them.

The author of this book does not dispense medical advice or prescribe the use of any technique as a form of treatment for physical, emotional, or medical problems without the advice of a physician, either directly or indirectly. The intent of the author is only to offer information of a general nature to help you in your quest for emotional and spiritual well-being. In the event you use any of the information in this book for yourself, which is your constitutional right, the author and the publisher assume no responsibility for your actions.

Any people depicted in stock imagery provided by Getty Images are models, and such images are being used for illustrative purposes only.
Certain stock imagery © Getty Images.

ISBN: 978-1-9822-4807-9 (sc)
ISBN: 978-1-9822-4808-6 (e)

Print information available on the last page.

Balboa Press rev. date: 07/21/2020

TABLE OF CONTENTS

Dear Speaking and Imaging Participant,

I am so delighted you are taking this program! Congratulations on your decision. I assure you, you will not be sorry--nervous on occasion perhaps, but not sorry. Of all the courses I have taught in the public, private, and corporate sectors, this is by far my favorite.

Many years ago, I read the story about Mark Edlund, a young man who lost his life in Vietnam. When his special effects were returned to his parents, they found a yellowed, crisply folded paper in his wallet. He had carried it with him since 7th grade. That one day so many years ago, his teacher asked the class to write the names of every student in class on the left side of the paper. She then asked them to write one good thing about that person next to their name. That weekend, she took everyone's lists and made each student a copy of all of the good things their classmates had written about them. Mark Edlund had kept that paper with him all of these years as had many of his classmates who attended his funeral.

This story is significant because of the impact those words had on this young man and his classmates. These weeks will have a similar impact on you. At the end of the course, each student will receive all of the positive comments from fellow students about every talk he or she had given.

Compared to physics, math or Spanish, this program will indeed seem easy; however, you will learn far more than speaking skills. You will experience an entirely different outlook on life, especially regarding who is responsible for how you feel, how you act, how you react.

You will learn to see people differently. You will learn how to "read" people and become aware of how you are "read." You will learn how to use your voice to produce the greatest effect. In other words, you will have the opportunity to mold yourself as you want to be.

While you may eventually forget facts and figures learned elsewhere, you will undoubtedly retain much of what you master in this seminar, because you will have constant opportunities to be on your feet and apply those things you have learned.

You will also have many opportunities to laugh, cry, and genuinely feel good. Let me share with you the essence of one testimonial I received from a very bright, articulate young lady who was a naturally good speaker when she began the class.

She stated that she felt this course had done much more for her than she had ever expected. She said it had not just made her a better speaker, but it had made her a better person overall. She said she now feels more confident in her skills to relate to other people on a daily basis.

She said she would recommend this class to everyone because the lessons they will learn they will carry with them throughout their lives. She went on to say that she never would have thought that she would get this much from a class where she could talk a lot and there was no final exam. (Correction: there is a final exam, but it's one for which you can easily prepare.)

She said that the final and probably most important skill that she had learned in class was to only look for the positives in people. She said that picking out the good in people instead of bad has become second nature to her. She stated that this skill not only makes other people feel better, but it also reflects itself on her own disposition. When a person learns to see the positive in other people, it brings a much more peaceful, optimistic outlook to the rest of the world around them.

Another testimonial is quite different. This came from a very quiet, shy gal who was barely audible when she first addressed the class. Watching her with her head bowed and her eyes on the floor, I feared I had a real challenge ahead of me. I should not have worried, however, because her peers provided her with the support and validation that buoyed her and literally transformed her into an extremely effective speaker--one who touched our hearts with her words.

This young lady said that this Speaking class was the first class in school that she felt she actually got something out of it. She stated there were no words to explain how she loved it. She used to despise talking in front of the class. Now she views that prospect as a way to speak her mind freely. She said she felt that this class showed her a whole new level of confidence she never knew she had. Even though she would get nervous before her talks, she would get this feeling of excitement when she went to talk in front of the class. She also stated that this is the first time she actually liked going to a class in school. This class also gave her an idea of what she wanted to do as a career.

Not only did she learn how to talk effectively, she learned that she is a strong, confident, and unique individual. She realized this through hearing the reactions of her peers. She was so appreciative of lessons she learned about life.

You will find that you will probably fall somewhere in-between these two examples, and that is fine. Just practice your talks and enjoy each and every day of the class.

Good luck and have fun!!

Best wishes,

Gail H. Cassidy

Date _____   TOPIC _____

SELF EVALUATION
(WORST) 1, 3, 5, 7, 9, 10 (BEST)

	1	3	5	7	10
1. Nervousness before speaking					
2. Nervousness while speaking					
3. Nervousness after speaking					
4. Knowledge of topic					
5. Degree of preparation					
6. Audience interest					
7. Quality of voice					
8. Use of body					
9. Awareness of audience					
10. Enjoyment					

Make 14 copies of this page and evaluate yourself immediately after each presentation you give.

ADOPT AS YOUR PERSONAL MOTTO:

PREPARE, PRACTICE, AND DELIVER

THE TEN WORST HUMAN FEARS
(in the U.S.)

1. Speaking before a group

2. Heights

3. Insects and bugs

4. Financial problems

5. Deep water

6. Sickness

7. Death

8. Flying

9. Loneliness

10. Dogs

*David Wallechinsky, et al.: *The Book of Lists*. New York: Wm. Morrow & Co., Inc. 1977.

EFFECTIVE SPEAKING

RULES:

1. Be yourself.

2. Be prepared.

3. Know your audience.

4. Be clear on the **PURPOSE** of your talk.

5. Be clear on the **RESULT YOU DESIRE** from the audience.

6. **HAVE FUN!!!**

FIRST IMPRESSIONS

It takes only four seconds to form an opinion. You only have one chance to make a good first impression.

SUGGESTIONS:

When you walk to the front of the room to speak,

- Look out at the audience and use "soft eyes" when making eye contact for the first time. This allows the audience to "feel" your warmth.
- Look down as you place your notes on the podium.
- Feel the audience's anticipation.
- Pause long enough for the audience to respond.

Now, when they are with you,

- "Thanks for inviting me . . ."
- "I'm delighted to be here . . ."
- "I understand your organization . . ."
- "On the way here today I. . ."
- "I've been asked to speak to you today about . . ."
- Three out of four people . . ."
- "The president of the United States confirmed . . ."
- "How many of you are fearful of . . ."

Now you can move from behind the podium

Remember:

Know yourself, Know your material, Know your audience

NAME: _____   DATE: _____

PLANNING SHEET FOR PRESENTATIONS YOUR

PURPOSE IN MAKING THIS PRESENTATION:

_____

_____

_____

OPENING: (Use exact wording) _____

_____

_____

POINT #1: _____

   EVIDENCE: _____

_____

_____

POINT #2: _____

   EVIDENCE: _____

_____

_____

(you may only have one type of evidence, such as a story, for a two-minute talk)

POINT #3: _____

   EVIDENCE: _____

_____

_____

POINT #4: _____

   EVIDENCE: _____

_____

_____

CLOSE: (Use exact wording) _____

_____

MORAL: _____

_____

RESULT YOU DESIRE FROM AUDIENCE: _____

_____

NERVOUSNESS TOOL KIT

". . . the only thing we have to fear is fear itself."
-Franklin D. Roosevelt

Even professionals get nervous. Nervousness stimulates speakers to give superb performances.

BEFORE TALK:

1. Write down why you are nervous.

2. Talk to your nervousness, i.e.,
Nervous self: *What if I forget what I was going to say?*
Sane self: *You stop, look at your notes, then continue.*
Nervous self: *What if everyone notices?*
Sane self: *Then they notice.*
• Everyone forgets something some time in their lives. The audience will understand.
• Continue talking in your head to counter every reason you have listed for being nervous.

3. Repeat a positive affirmation three times, i.e., "I love my topic" or "I'm totally prepared" or "I'm relaxed and confident."
• "This is the best speech I've ever given."
• "People will love hearing what I have to say."
• "I am more and more relaxed every time I speak."
• BELIEVE WHAT YOU ARE SAYING TO YOURSELF.
• SAY IT EMPHATICALLY.

4. Feel warmth toward your audience.
• Feel joy in your stomach, like a roller coaster ride.
• Smile and activate that feeling of joy.

ABOUT TO GIVE TALK: Remember, a certain amount of fear is good.

1. ISOMETRICS: Clasp your fingers together in your lap. Squeeze as hard as you can. Then relax. The tension from the exercise and the upcoming talk will dissipate. Yul Brenner, a Broadway actor who performed 10,000 performances of "The King and I"

pressed up against a wall before each performance in order to release his nervousness.

2. **DIAPHRAGMATIC BREATHING:** As you are seated, take a deep breath, pushing stomach outward. Take three deep breaths and you will find your mental clarity improved--more oxygen to the brain.

3. **QUICK RELAXATION TECHNIQUE:** After deep breaths, visualize the most relaxing scene you can think of. Visualize it in detail and feel yourself begin to relax into the scene.

4. **PHYSICAL TECHNIQUE:** In the restroom, stand tall and then let yourself bend at the waist to the floor, like a rag doll. Relax into this position and then, one vertebra at a time, slowly come back up.

5. **ATTITUDE:** Choose the attitude you want.
   • Control your thoughts, e.g., positive affirmations.
   • Give up the idea of perfection. Being effective is about the impact your message has on the audience.

REMEMBER: You know more about what you are going to say than anyone in the audience. **ENJOY YOURSELF!!!**

CRITIQUE

PRESENTER

1. <u>Posture</u>: poised, confident, natural, and sincere
2. <u>Body language</u>: gestures, posture, hands, animation, open
3. <u>Voice</u>: volume, projection, tone, variation, enunciation, effective use of pause, conversational, warm, respectful
4. <u>Facial Expression</u>: congruent, use of eyes, use of expressions, great eye contact, "warm eyes"
5. <u>Enthusiasm</u>: forceful, concise, friendly, pleasant, natural, vibrant
6. <u>Appearance</u>: appropriate, professional, neat, groomed, polished

PRESENTATION

7. Catchy opening
8. Organization of material
9. Knowledge of subject
10. Positive feeling projected
11. Ideas clearly presented
12. Drew mental pictures
13. Clarified material
14. Avoided jargon/acronyms
15. Effective use of visuals
16. Strong closing
17. Creative
18. Effective use of questions
19. Involved audience
20. Clear purpose
21. Use of audience

IMPACT ON AUDIENCE

22. Thought-provoking, inspiring, convincing, challenging, enlightening, humorous, motivating, informative, fun
23. Showed awareness of audience needs, sincere
24. Inspired audience
25. Empathetic to audience
26. Made audience feel special
27. Conveyed emotion and excitement about subject
28. Aroused emotion in audience
29. Called attention to audience member
30. Made a difference.

PRESENTATION ASSIGNMENTS

PRESENTATION #1 - "Introduction" - A one-minute or less talk about the person you interviewed.

PRESENTATION #2 - "Favorite Funny Story" - Your first 2-minute Talk.

        Examples: Uncle Sam who taught you how to ski, Aunt Nancy who worked with you on algebra, your mom who made the best cakes, your friend who helped you with a project. etc.

PRESENTATION #3 - "Negotiating/Role Playing" - You will be given a role to play without understanding the other persons' points of view. In small groups you will play your role and then give a **1-minute** evaluation of task. . 1 minutes.

PRESENTATION #4 - "My Most Embarrassing Moment" - What is a lesson you learned as a result of your embarrassing moment? Examples: crashing while skiing on a too-steep slope, going out without parent's permission, doing something you should not have, forgetting to do an assignment and ramifications, getting into a fight with sibling, getting a ticket, trying to do too many things at the same time. This is a **2 minute talk.**

PRESENTATION #5 - "What I Know to Be True Talk" - 3-MINUTE TALK TO INFORM AUDIENCE ABOUT WHAT YOU KNOW TO BE TRUE. NOTICE THE ADDITION OF ONE MINUTE TO YOUR TALK.
Examples: What do you know more about than most people do? Are you informed about different types of music, swing dance, ham radio, hip hop, and/or hobbies that others may not be familiar with? If so, what do you know to be true about these? Make sure you include a story.

PRESENTATION # 6 - "Storytelling" - Come prepared to tell a **two-minute story** and a brief appropriate joke.

PRESENTATIONS #7 - "Show and Tell" (1 minute) & "Annoyance Talk" (2 minutes) - Show and Tell Talk (No preparation sheet necessary) Look for something you are particularly proud of: a trophy, an article in the paper about you or your dog or family member, a special pen you use, a special gift, an award of some sort--anything that you can use as a prop in your story next session.
"Annoyance Talk" Tell about a time when something happened that really made you angry, i.e., getting in the wrong grocery line, being cut off while driving, being accused of something you didn't

do, failing a test you studied for, losing something, etc..

PRESENTATION #8 - "Sales Presentation" - (2 minutes). You will sell a product and use the outline on the Sales Presentation Preparation sheet.

PRESENTATION #9 - "Talk to Entertain" - (2 minutes). • You may work together for this assignment. Each participant is required to fulfill a 2 minute segment • No preparation sheet necessary • Find a play or story to tell the group.
• Notes may be used but no reading is allowed.

PRESENTATION #10 - "Talk to Persuade" - (4 minutes). • Select a cause/issue you feel strongly about and persuade class to your way of thinking. • Use a variety of types of evidence
• Complete Planning Sheet indicating forms of evidence to be used.

PRESENTATION #11 - "Reading" - (2 minutes). • Mark your copy carefully. Refer to "Reading" (page 30) in your packets.

PRESENTATION #12 - "Tips Talk" - (2 minutes). Using the commitment you made many sessions ago from your tips booklet, "Be the Best That You Can Be," report on the outcome of applying your chosen tip.

PRESENTATION #13 - Review Your Packets carefully before class.
Essay due last session: 5 paragraphs, typed, double spaced on "Of What Value Was this Speak Well and Create the Image You Desire Class to Me?" Please construct this in the same manner you have constructed your talks. See a Planning sheet for ideas.
• Do not include a discussion of the instructor
• You may include recommendations for future changes in the course, if you desire.
• You may share your reactions about the change in a fellow classmate(s).

PRESENTATION #14 - FINAL EXAM (5 minutes) - See instructions on your Final Examination in your packets, page .

PRESENTATION "MUSTS"

1. Know your material thoroughly and have a clear focus on your topic.

2. Feel really good about the subject you are about the present. Be enthusiastic!

3. REMEMBER: The audience "mirrors" you. If you have fun presenting, your audience will have fun listening. KNOW YOUR AUDIENCE!

4. Create an emotional experience during your talk. Our lives are created by feeling, not by thought. Have audience experience your passion and excitement and they will remember your talk.

5. Two things an audience does not forgive:
   a. A speaker's lack of preparation (they interpret it as an insult).
   b. A negative, "I don't care" attitude projected by the speaker.

Effective Speaking is a skill where PREPARATION and ATTITUDE are apparent almost immediately.

RECOMMENDATIONS:

6. a. Avoid dairy before speaking. It can cause mucus in throat.
   b. When of age, don't drink any alcoholic beverages ever before speaking.
   You could be very embarrassed if you do.
   c. Don't overeat before speaking. You may have to burp during your talk.

7. Do not memorize your talk. Do not try to be perfect. No one is.

8. To guarantee yourself a great start, **memorize your opening sentence and your closing sentence.**

9. PRACTICE, PRACTICE, PRACTICE. Rehearse in front of a mirror.

10. Visualize giving your talk. See yourself relaxed and successful.

11. Welcome a tinge of anxiety. It is a sign you will be on your toes to do the best job you possibly can do. You are in good company.

Willard Scott, Diane Sawyer, plus numerous actors and broadcasters have experienced first-rate nervousness. How do you overcome it? Face the thing you fear, and fear will disappear.

12.   HINT: Number your note cards or pages of your talk--just in case...

13.   EYE COMMUNICATION: The eyes are the windows to the soul. They communicate attitude and emotions not spoken. Eyes show your outlook on life and are a barometer of your feelings. They are the only organ in your body that cannot lie. Eye communication is an integral part of the way we all talk to each other.

14.   PAUSES: Pauses are an effective method to get attention. Nothing is louder than silence. When you are silent for a moment the audience will hear that silence and put their attention on you. Pauses allow the audience to focus on you.

15.   POSITIVE ATTITUDE: It is felt by the audience. PA is associated with energy and enthusiasm. PA is associated with confidence. A charismatic person is almost always defined as being positive and enthusiastic.

16.   SMILE: It warms a room.

17.   PASSION: Tom Peter says "Forget all the convention 'rules' but one. There is one golden rule: Stick to topics you deeply care about and do not keep your passion buttoned inside your vest. An audience's biggest turn on is the speaker's obvious enthusiasm. If you are lukewarm about the issue, forget it!"

Jeff Walling says "If you can say it without passion, spare your voice and leave me a note."

Above all, HAVE FUN!

PLANNING SHEET FOR
NEGOTIATING/ROLE PLAYING

WHAT IS YOUR POSITION?: _____

_____

WHAT IS THE VALUE OF THIS TO THIS AUDIENCE?: _____

_____

OPENING: (Use exact wording) _____

_____

_____

EVIDENCE TO VALIDATE YOUR POSITION: _____

1. _____

#2: _____

#3: _____

#4: _____

#5: _____

CLOSE: (Use exact wording)_____

_____

POINT: _____

BENEFIT TO LISTENERS IN KNOWING HOW TO DO THIS:

_____

_____

_____

CASE STUDY:
PROBLEMS AT THE "Y"

from perspective of
ALICE, THE DAYCARE WORKER

Alice is a daycare worker with a "Y" located about 45 minutes from her home. A well-qualified person, she is newly employed and knows she has to make a good impression.

Unfortunately, this morning before work, Alice woke up late because the electricity went out during the night. On top of that, the shower ran only ice cold water. On the way to work, Alice was trying to make up for lost time and was stopped by the police and given a very high fine ticket plus points for exceeding the speed limit by 20 miles.

Alice arrives at work late. Her supervisor is unhappy not only because Alice is late, but also because two other daycare workers called in sick and she cannot find replacements, and today is "parent's day" where Mom and Dad come in to see how their little child is doing in nursery school. Alice has to double her workload for the day.

The first person to arrive at the "Y" is Mrs. Van Dyke whom everyone is familiar with. She is a regular and is a complainer about everything associated with the "Y" even though she comes daily. Alice politely takes care of her but loses time listening to Mrs. Van Dyke's complaints.

By eleven o'clock Alice has seen numerous parents, is exhausted and the parents are lining up complaining because they've been waiting so long. When Joe Smith arrives at the counter and starts being verbally abusive, Alice explodes and tells him a thing or two. Alice's supervisor overhears the tirade and asks Alice to come in the back.

What should Alice do?

PROBLEMS AT THE "Y"

from perspective of
<u>JOE, THE PARENT</u>

Joe Smith is the father of five young children. His wife died recently from cancer, and he is devastated. He is an iron worker who cannot depend on continuous employment and lives in constant fear of not being able to care for his children.

This morning Joe was at work when a coworker dropped a heavy piece of metal on Joe's knee as he was bending to weld an iron joist. Joe's pain is surpassed only by his fear of being laid up and unable to earn money and his fear of disappointing his kids in daycare.

He arrived at the "Y" at 8:30 a.m. for his parent/teacher interview. It is now after 11:00 a.m., and still no one has even called his name. This cool-looking, pretty daycare worker is taking her sweet time making idle chitchat with other parents as he sits there in pain, losing precious time off the job.

Enough is enough. At 11:05 after watching the idle chitchat continue, Joe hobbles up to the desk and lets them know what he thinks in no uncertain terms. That sassy broad has nerve to answer him back in that tone of voice!

What should Joe do?

PROBLEMS AT THE "Y"

from perspective of
<u>MRS. JONES, THE SUPERVISOR</u>

Today started like any other. Mrs. Jones got the kids off to school and got to work in plenty of time. Unfortunately, there were two messages for her. Two of the scheduled daycare workers called in sick. Mrs. Jones phoned her list of substitutes but could find no one at home. Worse things could happen, she thought.

Mrs. Jones had great confidence in the new girl, Alice, and the rest of the staff. It would be tough, but they would get through the day.

The "Y" opens and the new girl, Alice, is not yet there. Normally, Mrs. Jones would not be that upset, but this early in the day is a very bad time to have parents backing up, especially on this special teacher/parent day. Alice arrived in a harried state, apologized and started to work immediately.

At 11:05, Mrs. Jones hears loud, abusive language from a very angry man, followed by equally loud, abusive language from her new hiree, Alice.

What should Mrs. Jones do?

EVALUATION

Looking at "Be the Best That You Can Be" tips booklet, find tips that would be applicable to this situation.

Review reasons why Joe is right.

Review reasons why supervisor is right.

Review reasons why Alice is right.

How should this situation be handled? All of the scenes have occurred, now how can Joe be placated? Alice? Mrs. Jones? Is it possible?

Act out the next scene, with the goal of placating all three people.

ORGANIZATION OF TALKS

Dottie Walters, a renown speaker and trainer of speakers, recommends what she calls the "five finger" talk. The opening is the pinky, three points, and end with a strong thumb.

Keeping that image in mind, be mindful of what every talk must have to be effective.

1. OPENING: See examples on Openings Page You need to capture your audience's attention immediately with a catchy opening.

2. UP TO THREE POINTS: Use evidence (See Evidence Sheet) to **prove your point.** Use a story, statistics, quotes--whatever is necessary to bring your point home to the audience.

3. CLOSE includes three parts:
     1• State ACTION audience should take. Why else would you be talking to them? You want them to take action, even if your intent is to entertain, their action is laughter.
     2• Restate your point and action needed.
     3• State benefit to those listening to your talk. The following is an example:

TALK

OPENING: Road rage has the potentially grave consequences. "It's important to see things from other people's perspective.

POINT WITH EVIDENCE: About a month ago, I was driving to work, when all of a sudden a van passed me on the right side, got in front of me, and slammed on the brakes. I almost slammed into him. I was so angry I wanted to swear at him or better yet, tap his fender and see how he liked it.   We came to a dead stop. People got out of their cars--the perfect opportunity to tell this man what I thought of his driving skills. Fortunately, I held my tongue because what I could not see was a young boy who had run out into the street to get his ball and had been grazed by the car in front of the van. I also quickly learned that this man had been so impatient because he was trying to get his vastly pregnant wife to the hospital before it was too late. I am so glad I did not act on my initial impulse."

CLOSING:
     1.   (Here is the ACTION the audience should take.)

2. RESTATE POINT AND ACTION. Restate point: *"My point is: See things from another's perspective."*

3. BENEFIT: (Here is the third step, the benefit the listeners will receive by doing what is asked for in the POINT STEP.)
"Because if you do, you may prevent considerable embarrassment."

(Please note that this talk contained a specific incident out of the class member's life; the speaker asked for action; and then gave a benefit for the listeners resulting from this action.)

Let's Examine the Steps of the Speaking Formula

1. OPENING: You need to capture your audience's attention immediately with a catchy opening.

2. UP TO THREE POINTS: Use evidence (See Evidence Sheet) to **prove your point.** Use a story *(Should be an experience from your own life--one that taught you a lesson)*, statistics, quotes--whatever is necessary to bring your point home to the audience. *Allow the audience to know immediately what your point is.*

3. CLOSE includes three parts:
    1• State ACTION audience should take. Why else would you be talking to them? You want them to take action, even if your intent is to entertain, their action is laughter.

    2• Restate your POINT (Answers the question: *What do you want us to do (that you think will help us?)* and **action needed.**

    3• State BENEFIT to those listening to your talk. Answers the question: *Why should we do it? (How will we benefit if we do what you ask? e.g., what's in it for me?)*

OPENINGS

(Can also be used throughout talk to get audience's attention)

- TALK OBJECTIVES:
  - To inform
  - To entertain
  - To persuade
  - To inspire

- Tell them what you are going to tell them.

- Startling statement: "Look to your right and left. One will not be here by the end of the semester."

- Quote an authority: "The fire captain said the most common area for fires is the kitchen."

- Use a prop. If selling, show your product. If a prop relates to your talk, use it.

- Compliment your audience. Find out something special about the group and relate it to them.

- Ask a question. Rhetorical: "Are you afraid of losing your job?" Direct: "How many of you have slept through your alarm?"

- Ask your audience to do something. "Stretch. Introduce yourself to the person next to you. Stand."

- Tell a story or joke (if you can).

- Show a graphic on an overhead.

PURPOSE:
1. To get an immediate response from your audience.
2. To release tension.
3. To build confidence.
4. To get a perspective on your audience by their responses.

EVIDENCE

CITING AN EXPERT: Quoting someone in authority.

FACTS/STATISTICS: Numbers, comparisons, percentages.

PROPS: A visual, picture, object, drawing, etc.

ACTION: Act out how something works

METAPHORS: Making a direct comparison. Relate to something to which audience can relate, i.e., *the car skidded the length of a football field.*

STORIES: A story about something that has happened to you or to someone you know.

There are different types of stories you can use:

• **Vignettes:** brief, descriptive incident or scene which can be told in a minute or so. Historical events, examples, case studies.
• **Life and death stories:** stories of great loss, hardship, or pain. Olympic athletes, cancer survivors, people who have overcome incredible odds tell their stories. These stories deal with life and death and can be used to teach a profound lesson.
• **Embarrassing moment story:** Funny stories which allow us to be funny. Use to humanize yourself so audience can identify with you.
• **News stories:** Current events that can be used to prove your point and which add to your credibility.
• **Personal stories:** Ordinary experiences that prove your point.
adapted from Doug Stevenson's *Never Be Boring Again!*

PEOPLE LOVE STORIES!!

MORE ON STORIES AS EVIDENCE

Using a story as evidence has worked well for a number of famous speakers. Dale Carnegie employed stories when he gave a talk at the YMCA early in his career after he had exhausted his topic and still had time left. He told a story about his topic, and his speech was remembered, and Carnegie went on to build an empire on speaking.

In a *Network Marketing Lifestyles* (July 2001) article, the headline reads "The cornerstone of Gove's teaching is simple--the key to making a good presentation is to make a point and tell a story. [Bill] Gove is masterful at it; his comedic timing is impeccable. Says Gove, 'I never look at myself as a public speaker. . . sounds an awful lot like a government job. I like being known as a storyteller.'"

The article goes on to say that "each story has a life of its own. it might be only three or four minutes long, but each one has a premise, a problem, and a payoff or lesson learned--just like a regular speech. We learn to connect mini-speeches together, rather than face the horrible task of sitting down and organizing one long 40-minute speech.

"This approach comes from Mark Twain . . . It's, 'Let me tell you a story,' and then, part way into the story, you say, 'Let me give you an example. . .' - and of course, the example is always the personal story."

Similar to Carnegie, Gove came across his style accidentally. His boss announced that he was going to present a half-hour speech on closing the sale. Gove was terrified. "I thought--'You must be crazy! A half hour on closing?' I didn't think I could come up with more than ten minutes' worth. I was wrong; it was worse. I put together my talk on closing--and it came out to about five minutes. . . so I added 25 minutes of Uncle Phil's stories.' The talk was a sensation. Twenty-five minutes of Maine vignettes a la Uncle Phil wrapped around a central theme ("closing the sale") gave Bill Gove the platform for a lifetime of stories that teach and train as they entertain."

The point is audiences tune out to "thou shalts" but tune in to a good story. Stories can be supplemented with statistics, analogies, etc., but it is the story and the point that they will remember.

CLOSINGS

- **CHOOSE CLOSING ACCORDING TO OBJECTIVE OF TALK.**

- Tell them what you told them. (Summary of main points)

- Ask audience to take action.

- Challenge the audience to take a specific action, e.g., contribute to a charity, floss daily, be careful on the slopes, take care of your parents...

- Refer to your opening statement. This ties the talk together.

- Dramatize your point.

- Restate the key benefit of your talk.

- Ask a rhetorical question.

- Use an appropriate quotation.

- Make an observation.

- Give a final motivating statement.

- Combine techniques.
    - Tell a story
    - Recite a poem
    - Quote someone in authority

"Wind up with a line, or anecdote, a proverb, a quotation or some other memorable piece of copy that leaves your audience laughing or thoughtful--depending on the subject of your address." from *How To Be the Life of the Podium* by Sylvia Simmons.

CLOSE SHOULD TRIGGER AUDIENCE APPLAUSE

ENJOY THE ACCOLADES!!

AFFIRMATIONS

To counter nervousness, it is essential to understand that you can *drown out* the discouraging silent voices that often speak in your mind—those voices that make you doubt yourself and make you feel incapable of speaking in front of a group. We get what we focus on emotionally. Focus on a relaxed, dynamic presentation.

To use an Affirmation, just speak ALOUD to yourself. Carefully plan each word you want to hear. State the words clearly and concisely. Speak them with authority as though you are lecturing an audience of hundreds who have come to hear your words of wisdom, e.g., "I am a dynamic speaker!" "The audience will love my talk!" "I am totally prepared!" "I am confident!" Expect success and you will be successful.

Painting this picture in your mind's eye will give you the feeling of confidence. The words will follow. Act "as if" you already have positive, confident thoughts, and they will follow. In your mind's eye, see the audience responding well to your talk.

Persistence in using Affirmations and visualizing them in your mind's eye will prove highly rewarding. Assign yourself daily "private time" for this exercise. Each day it will become easier until it will be picked up by habit and become "you" without conscious thought.

Norman Vincent Peale said, **"You are not what you think you are, but what you think, you are."** Think about that!

Adapted from an article by Robert J. White, *Think and Grow Rich Newsletter.*

NAME: _____   DATE: _____

PLANNING SHEET FOR
MY MOST EMBARRASSING MOMENT

WHAT MOMENT ARE YOU GOING TO TALK ABOUT?: _____
_____

WHAT IS THE VALUE OF THIS TO THIS AUDIENCE?: _____
_____
_____
_____

OPENING: (Use exact wording) _____
_____
_____
_____

STEPS IN MOMENT:
1. _____

#2: _____

#3: _____

#4: _____

CLOSE: (Use exact wording) _____
_____
_____

POINT: _____

BENEFIT TO LISTENERS IN KNOWING HOW TO DO THIS: _____
_____
_____
_____
_____

THE BLIND MEN AND THE ELEPHANT

It was six men of Indostan
To learning much inclined,
Who went to see the Elephant
(Though all of them were blind),
That each by observation
Might satisfy his mind.
The First approached the Elephant,
And happening to fall
Against his broad and sturdy side,
At once began to bawl:
"God bless me! but the Elephant
Is very like a wall!"
The Second, feeling of the tusk,
Cried, "Ho! what have we here
So very round and smooth and sharp?
To me 'tis mighty clear
This wonder of an Elephant
Is very like a spear!"
The Third approached the animal,
And happening to take
The Squirming trunk within his hands,
Thus boldly up he spake:
"I see," quoth he, "the Elephant
Is very like a snake!"
The Fourth reached out an eager hand,
And felt about the knee
"What most this wondrous beast is like
Is might plain," quoth he:
"Tis clear enough, the Elephant
Is very like a tree!"
The Fifth who chanced to touch the ear,
Said: "E'en the blindest man
Can tell what this resembles most;
Deny the fact who can,
This marvel of an Elephant
Is very like a fan!"
The Sixth no sooner had begun
About the beast to grope,
Then seizing on the swinging tail
That fell within his scope,
"I see," quoth he, "the Elephant
Is very like a rope!"
And so these men of Indostan
Disputed loud and long,
Each in his own opinion
Exceeding stiff and strong,
Though each was partly in the right,
And all were in the wrong!

-John Godfrey Saxe

BODY LANGUAGE CUES

WHAT <u>COULD</u> THE FOLLOWING GESTURES MEAN?

1. Tapping of fingers
2. Shrugging of shoulders
3. Wringing of hands
4. Clenched fist(s)
5. Open hands, palms up, in front of body
6. Arms crossed on chest
7. Walking fast, chin held high, arms swinging
8. Shuffling walk, head low
9. Palm held to cheek
10. Stroking chin
11. Touching, rubbing nose
12. Hands on Hips

13. Head tilted to side
14. Steepling of hands
15. Peering over glasses
16. Pacing
17. Pinching bridge of nose
18. Sitting on edge of chair
19. Crossed kicking leg
20. Pointing of index finger
21. Poor eye contact
22. Sideways glance
23. Unbuttoned coat
24. Rubbing eyes
25. Playing with hair
26. Hand covering mouth

NEXT TO EACH NUMBER, WRITE THE FIRST LETTER OF WHAT EACH ACTION REPRESENTS TO YOU, USING THE FOLLOWING AS A GUIDE:

(D) - Defensiveness
(S) - Suspicion
(C) - Confidence
(F) - Frustration

(R) - Reflective
(O) - Openness and Cooperation
(I) - Insecurity and Nervousness

**Notice how many different meanings each could have.
Body language cues are one part of the message.**

VOICE

If people perceive a discrepancy between what you say and how you say it, they will believe your voice. For example, if you see a tie you hate and say, "Nice tie, Joe" you could clearly be insulting him by your voice even though your words are perfect. The following six methods will help bring your voice and words into alignment:

• **BREATH CONTROL:** The more breath control you have, the more power you voice has. One way to learn to control how you breathe is to lie on a bed and put a book on your abdomen. If you are breathing correctly, the book should go up and down. (Remember our diaphragmatic breathing exercises.) To increase breathing control, take a deep breath, then exhale as you count to five. Repeat, increasing the count until you're exhaling to the count of 10.

• **VOLUME:** Read your audience's body language to determine if your volume is appropriate. If your voice is too loud, people will pull away or cross their arms as if to protect themselves. If your voice is too soft, your listeners will strain forward to hear you. Deliberately lower your voice to give importance to information or to exercise authority. When you lower your voice, you force your listeners to focus on what you are saying.

• **PITCH:** If your voice is too high, it will convey youth or nervousness. To find a comfortably low pitch, start speaking at a high pitch and count to 10, lowering your pitch with each count. When you find a pitch you like, practice speaking at that pitch until it automatically lowers to the new level.

• **HESITATION:** See sheet on "Toward More Powerful Speech." Usually hesitation is due to running out of breath. The solution is to take deeper breaths and release the air slowly so that it will last until you reach a natural place to pause.

• **PACE:** Speaking too fast indicates nervousness or being hurried or you don't want to be bothered. Makes you seem unapproachable. If you speak too slowly, listeners think you aren't sure of yourself or your information. Put more energy behind your voice, shorten pauses, and move quickly over vowel sounds.

• **ENUNCIATION:** Poor enunciation is usually the result of tension. Relax your facial muscles by yawning, tensing and relaxing your shoulder and neck muscles. Remember: your voice conveys messages that may hurt or help

VOICE (continued)

your image.

from Joan Sered Smith's (with P.A. Haddock) article, "Speak up and be heard" in *Manager's Memo.*

- **RECOMMENDATIONS:**

USE A CONVERSATIONAL TONE. Speak "to," not "at" your audience--as if you were speaking to a friend. Perfection is out. Reality is in. Allow audience to *feel* that you, the speaker, are one of them. Your goal is to establish rapport with your audience.

• AVOID A MONOTONE; it's deadly. Hypnotists use a monotone in order to relax a client and enable the client to relax. You don't want that. Raising your pitch, then lowering it will snap listeners out of their reverie. Speeding up, slowing down, pausing are great ways to avoid the sleep-inducing monotone voice.

RELATE TO YOUR AUDIENCE

• Speak with *warm eyes*.

• Tell your audience something special about them.

• Be humble!

• Use the pronoun "we" rather than "you."

• Whenever appropriate, mention the names of <u>some</u> of your listeners. The rest of the audience will pay even closer attention.

• Enjoy giving your talk.

• Be yourself. Avoid jokes if you are not a naturally funny person.

• Be sincere.

• Talk in terms of your audience's interests.

• Make sure your body language is congruent with your message. Remember: 55% of all messages comes from your body, 38% from your voice.

• Know that you cannot <u>not</u> communicate.

• Smile.

• Communicate your genuine enthusiasm through your body and voice.

• Speak with a warm heart.

GUIDELINES

• **NOTECARDS:** Use 5x8 inch cards or 3x5 inch cards (if you want to keep them in your pocket) or an 8 1/2 x 11 inch sheet of paper folded lengthwise. Number your cards or pages in case you drop them.

• Do not write out your talks.

• Never memorize a talk word-for-word, except for opening and closing sentence.

• Have an opening that will grab your audience's attention.

• Use evidence to substantiate your points.

• Know your subject thoroughly.

• **PRACTICE. PRACTICE. PRACTICE.** Don't try to "wing" it.

• Use visual aids when appropriate

• Close strongly so that the audience will be left with a strong impression of your talk.

• Control "butterflies" by using

  • Isometrics

  • Diaphragmatic breathing

  • Deep breaths to enable you to relax and visualize

  • Affirmation to psyche yourself.

PLANNING SHEET

YOUR PURPOSE IN MAKING THIS PRESENTATION: _____

_____

OPENING: (Use exact wording) _____

_____

POINT #1: _____

  EVIDENCE: _____

_____

_____

POINT #2: _____

  EVIDENCE: _____

_____

____(you may only have one type of evidence, such as a story, for a two-minute talk)_____

POINT #3: _____

  EVIDENCE: _____

_____

_____

POINT #4: _____

  EVIDENCE: _____

_____

_____

CLOSE: (Use exact wording) _____

_____

MORAL: _____

BENEFIT TO LISTENERS: _____

HUMAN RELATIONS STACK

"Stacking" is a great mnemonic to remember items, names, dates, or points in a talk. Once you know the points you want to make, you then develop them into a picture. For example, if you wanted to remember 9 human relations principles, you could picture the following: The items underlined are those you want to clearly see.

In your mind's eye picture an <u>ice statue</u> of a <u>cheerleader</u> with <u>headphones</u> on. Look closely and you'll see, as in a cartoon, <u>bubbles</u> coming out of her head, indicating she is thinking. What she is thinking about is a <u>thermostat</u> so she won't melt. In her <u>praying hands</u> is a huge <u>candy bar</u>. On the wrapper of the candy bar is a big <u>C</u> and a <u>plus sign</u> (<u>+</u>).

The pictures are explained as follows:

<u>Ice Statue</u>: Accept people as they are.

<u>Cheerleader</u>: Be enthusiastic in all you do.

<u>Headphones</u>: Listen. It is the greatest compliment you can pay

someone.

<u>Bubbles</u>: Thoughts. "Change your thoughts and you change your

world."   -Emerson.

<u>Thermostat</u>: You can't control what happens to you, but you can

always control your reactions.

<u>Praying hands</u>: Accept what is, e.g., Serenity Prayer.

<u>Candy bar</u>: Treat others as you wish to be treated.

<u>C</u>: Do not criticize other people. No one ever appreciates it.

<u>+ sign</u>: Look for the positives in everyone.

Name _____   Date _____

TIPS TALK COMMITMENT SHEET

(Choose one of the TIPS in the "Best the Best That You Can Be" booklet to apply to the person of your choice.)

TIP CHOSEN:

WHY DID YOU CHOOSE THIS TIP?

PERSON WITH WHOM YOU EXPECT TO USE TIP:

ON WHAT SITUATION DO YOU THINK YOU CAN USE THIS TIP?

WHAT DO YOU HOPE WILL HAPPEN?

WHAT WILL YOU DO IF THE TIP DOES NOT WORK THE FIRST TIME?

HOW MANY TIMES WILL YOU ATTEMPT TO USE THIS TIP?

PLEASE NOTE: The result of this Commitment will be reported in SESSION12.

ENUNCIATION

A good voice commands respect and helps in holding your listeners' attention. A variety in pitch and increases and decreases in volume are essential in being a good storyteller. Also vitally important is articulation. Poor articulation arises from lazy lips, stiff jaws, or a thick, clumsy tongue.

To practice good articulation, read aloud three times the following tongue twisters. Record yourself on a tape recorder so you can hear how you sound.

1. She sells seashells down by the seashore.
2. She saw six slim, sleek, slender saplings.
3. Rubber baby buggy bumpers.
4. A big black bear ate a big black bug.
5. Sam shipped six slippery, slimy eels in separate crates.
6. The sixth sheik's sixth sheep's sick.
7. The sharp, shrill shriek of the bat shatters the shadowy silence.
8. Two terrible, tedious, tiresome talkers took advantage of the debating team.
9. The seething sea ceaseth and thus the seething sea sufficeth us.
10. Limber Lena leaped laughingly after Lazy Lally.

from *Basic Oral Communication, Fifth Edition*, Glenn R. Capp/Carol C. Capp, G. Richard Capp, Jr. Prentice Hall, Englewood Cliffs, NJ, 1990

Practice the following nursery rhyme three times. First, speak softly and slowly, making sure you clearly enunciate every vowel and consonant, then progress louder and faster for the last two times.

> Mary had a little lamb,
> Its fleece was white as snow;
> And everywhere that Mary went,
> The lamb was sure to go.
> It followed her to school one day,
> Which was against the rule;
> It made the children laugh and play,
> To see a lamb in school.

ENUNCIATION (continued)

To perfect your "th's" memorize and repeat Theopholis Thistle, the Thistle Sifter."

THEOPHOLIS THISTLE, THE THISTLE SIFTER

Theopholis Thistle, the Thistle Sifter, sifted a sieve of unsifted thistles, but where is the sieve of unsifted thistles that Theopholis Thistle, the Thistle Sifter sifted?

If you practice this a few times a day, you will be able to master the "th" sound.

ENTHUSIASM

"Forget all the conventional 'rules' but one. There is one golden rule: stick to topics you deeply care about and do not keep your passion buttoned inside your vest. An audience's biggest turn on is the speakers' obvious enthusiasm. If you are lukewarm about the issue, forget it!" - Tom Peters

Think of someone in your live whom you really admire, someone about whom you could say, "Now that's a real winner!" First, if you know this person personally, you will probably be able to say that this person also makes you feel good. We tend to admire those who make us feel special.

Who is this person? Is it one or both of your parents, a relative, a trainer, coach, or friend?

Why do you admire this person? What qualities does s/he have? Is he or she "energetic?" Is "positive" a word you would use? How about "loyal," "respected," "giving," "honest," "courageous," "kind?" And how about "enthusiastic?"

Let's take a look at these descriptive words. First of all, many of the words relate to values. Secondly, notice whether these descriptors are skills or attitudes? Most definitely they are attitudes, and there is no school that I know of that offers a course in attitude. Perhaps there should be.

The importance of attitude was discovered through a research study done by the Carnegie Foundation for the Advancement of Teaching and later substantiated by additional studies made at the Carnegie Institute of Technology. The findings of these studies revealed that even in technical professions about 15 percent of a person's financial success is due to his or her technical knowledge and about 85 percent is due to their people skills - to personality and attitude, e.g., 15 percent for aptitude; 85% for attitude! How true the old saw, "It's your attitude, not your aptitude, that determines your altitude."

How can you change your attitude? Decide to. As I've said before, "Fake it until you make it." Act and you will be.

There was a letter to "The Pinstriped Advisor," in an issue of *Executive Edge* newsletter, asking "What, if anything, can I do to be more charismatic? Or is charisma something you're born with and you either have it or you don't?"

Pinstriped Advisor had an excellent answer. He said Charisma is not a goal. It's a byproduct - of your passion and drive, of your commitment to ideas and people. It comes when you show courage and make sacrifices. It flows out of your caring and your honesty. Sure, these are old-fashioned words - but they're the qualities that make people devoted to you and willing to follow you.

So don't try to live somebody else's idea of charisma...Still, you can do things that will enhance your chances of being charismatic - or at least having influence over people. "Probably the most important thing you can do is to make a conscious effort to be more enthusiastic," says Philip H. Friedman, Ph.D., ...'You'll notice that no matter the person, those who we describe as charismatic are always enthusiastic. And it's their enthusiasm that affects people. So when you wake up, tell yourself you *will* be more enthusiastic. Psyche yourself up, visualize it and make a commitment to it by reminding yourself of the benefits that charisma will bring you.'"

Enthusiasm is an attitude. An attitude is a thought. And it's exciting to know that we can control our thoughts all day long, therefore, our attitudes, therefore, our level of enthusiasm. It's all there for the thought!

TOWARD MORE POWERFUL SPEECH

SUGGESTIONS	EXAMPLES	COMMENTS
Avoid hesitations.	"I *er* want to say that *ah* this one is *er* the best, *you know*."	Hesitations make one sound unprepared and uncertain.
Avoid uncertainly expressions.	"*Maybe* we could *perhaps* go there later. I *guess* we should. I *think* that is it."	Uncertainly expressions communicate a lack of commitment, direction, and conviction.
Avoid overpoliteness.	"*Excuse* me, *please, sir,*"	Overpolite forms signal one's subordinate status.
Avoid too many intensifiers.	"*Really,* this was *the greatest*; it was *truly phenomenal.*"	Too many intensifiers make one's speech all sound the same and do now allow for intensifying what should be emphasized.
Avoid simple one-word answers.	"*Yes; no; Ok; sure.*"	One-word answers may signal a lack of communication skills and a lack of interest and commitment.
Avoid disqualifiers.	"I *didn't read the entire article,* but...; I *didn't actually see the accident,* but..."	Disqualifiers signal a lack of competence.
Avoid disclaimers that express a lack of conviction or expertise.

validity. | "*I'm probably wrong about this,* but...; I *don't know anything about taxes,* but | Disclaimers deny responsibility for one's statements and may call into question their |
Avoid weak modifiers.	"This looks *pretty* good; I look this one, *kind of.*"	Weak modifiers make one seem unsure and indefinite.
Avoid tag questions.	"that was a great movie, *wasn't it?*; She's brilliant, *don't you think?*"	Weak modifiers make another's agreement and therefore signal one's need for agreement and one's own uncertainly.
Avoid self-critical	"*I'm not very good at*	Self-critical statements

statements.	this. This is my first public speech."	signal a lack of confidence and make public one's inadequacies.
Avoid cliches and "bromides."	"tried and true; few and far between; She's as pretty as a picture."	Cliches and bromides (phrases and sentences that have been worn out by too-frequent usage) signal a lack of originality and creativity and a reliance on stock phrases and sentences.
Avoid slang and vulgar expressions.	"##!!!///****; no problem!"	Slang and vulgarity signal low social class and hence little power.

DeVito, Joseph A. <u>The Interpersonal Communication Book</u>

NAME _____   Date: _____

SALES PRESENTATION
(USE BACK OF PAGE TO COMPLETE YOUR ANSWERS)
PLEASE USE NOTECARDS FOR YOUR ACTUAL PRESENTATION!!!

OPENING: **First sentence will be question bearing on a need.**
•Question bearing on a need of the listener(s), e.g., "If there were a way for you to totally relax and enjoy a rainy day (or whatever two things your product will do for the listener), is that something you would like to hear more about?" Write your exact question with the two benefits for the reader:_____

_____

_____.

ESTABLISH NEEDS:
•Why should listener(s) buy your product? What will it do for them?
•**List the benefits of buying your product** (or what the product will do for them):
1.
2.
3.
4.

SOLUTION:
•I would like to recommend _name of your product_ , because ____(use any of the reasons you have filled in listed below)
_____

WHY? List reasons why, e.g.,
       1. What the product is and how buyer can relate to it: _____

_____

       2. Why should they relate to product? _____

_____

       3. What is significance of product? _____

_____

       4. What feature(s) of your product can they use? _____

_____

       5. How will your product help solve their problems? _____
_____
       6. What is most exciting/outstanding about this product for you? _____
_____
•Write a brief, yet very strong, summary of why a person should buy your product. Then ask for them to buy it.

CLOSING SENTENCE:

SAMPLE OPENINGS, ACCORDING TO PRODUCT BEING SOLD:

COURSE: If loving what you do every day and earning money are important to you, would you be interested in learning about how this could occur?

CELL PHONE: If you could have clear reception and unlimited minutes to speak at a price you can afford, would you be interested in finding additional information on this product?

COMPUTER: If portability, reliability and low cost are important computer needs for you, would you like to see a demonstration?

TRAVEL AGENT: If your ideal vacation trip met your expectations at a low cost, would you be interesting in hearing more?

CAUSES/ISSUES
WOULD YOU FIGHT OR MARCH FOR ANY OF THESE?
(Choose one issue you would like to talk about)

Environment: Pollution - air and water
Education - quality
Health Care system made mandatory
Children's right to divorce parents - rights
The Homeless - rights
Energy - solar/nuclear
The Justice System - Victim's rights
Veterans: pensions, hospitalization
Nutrition: labeling laws, banning sugar
Politics: balanced budget, honesty
Campaign reform
Youth - curfews/laws
Three strikes you're out law
Small Business Tax Reform
Churches/synagogues - separation church/state
Spirituality: freedom of new age thinking
Public Safety issues
Infant protection
Child Care regulations
Home Health Care disabled
Tourism protection
Space Exploration
Animal Care & rights: vivisection
Literacy eradication
Civil Rights Issues
Fashion industry ripoffs
Books: Censorship
Movies: Censorship
Sport figures' salaries
CEO salaries
Federal tax equality
State sales tax
Local property taxes for education
Broadcasting responsibilities
Community Development
Research methods
Women's Issues
Honesty among politicians
Human Relation Principles
Loss of the Rain Forests

Family Issues
Media responsibilities/ sensationalism
Elderly: Medicare, S.S.
Discrimination: race, sex, age, etc.
Immigration: tighter regulations
Agriculture: pesticides
Parks & Recreation: overuse & abuse
Substance Abusers: Drunk drivers
Law: fairness of justice system today
School funding: equality rich/poor
Government bureaucracy
Political Fleecing of America
Road & Bridges repairs: dangers
Non-profit Agencies: gov't support
Censoring the Internet
Handicapped legislation
Human Development Programs
Megan's Law
Justice System: equality/fairness
Water Rights
Defense budget
Balanced budget
Unions
Gay rights
Sexuality Issues
Art censorship
Music lyrics: censorship/responsibility
Corporate Downsizing
Food contamination
Gun laws - The Brady Law
Construction laws
Air bags on passenger side
Real Estate development
Religion
Late term abortions
Cloning human beings
War
Civility
Kindness
Sincerity

LIST OTHER CAUSES AND/OR ISSUES YOU FEEL STRONGLY ABOUT THAT YOU WOLD RATHER TALK ABOUT:

List adapted from The Path by Laurie Beth Jones.

NAME _____   Date: _____

PERSUASION TALK
(USE BACK OF PAGE TO COMPLETE YOUR ANSWERS)
PLEASE USE NOTECARDS FOR YOUR ACTUAL PRESENTATION!!!

OPENING: First sentence will be a statement or question to challenge your audience toyour way of thinking._____

_____

_____

ESTABLISH REASONS:
• Why should listener(s) believe in your point of view? What will it do for them?
• List the benefits of buying-in to your belief (or what will it do for them):
1.
2.
3.
4.

SOLUTION:
• I would like to recommend _____, because _____ (use any of the reasons you have filled in listed below)
WHY? List reasons why, e.g.,

  1. What your belief is and how listener can relate to it: _____

  _____

  2. Why should they relate to your belief? _____

  _____

  3. What is significance of your belief? _____

  _____

  4. How will your belief(s) help solve their problems? _____

  5. What is most exciting/outstanding about your beliefs for you?

  _____

• Write a brief, yet very strong, summary of why a person believe you. Then ask for them to agree with you.

CLOSING SENTENCE:

READING

Using a pen, mark your copy with the following symbols so you can read effortlessly and with meaning when you address the class.

•For a brief pause, use a slash (/) between words.
•For a full stop, such as the end of a sentence, use an x (X).
•To indicate a group of words should be said in one breath, underline the words in one straight line.
•If certain individual words are to be emphasized or punched, double underline them to remind you as you are reading.

PRACTICE THE FOLLOWING:

Four score and seven years ago / our fathers brought forth on this continent/ a new nation,/conceived in Liberty,/ and dedicated to the proposition that all men are created equal.X

Now we are engaged in a great civil war,/ testing whether that nation,/ or any nation/ so conceived and so dedicated,/ can long endure.X We are met on a great battlefield of that war.X We have come to dedicate a portion of that field/ as a final resting-place/ for those/ who here/ gave their lives/ that that nation might live.X It is altogether fitting and proper/ that we should do this, etc.X

WRITING ASSIGNMENT

ESSAY DUE NEXT WEEK

Please write a five-paragraph, typed, double spaced essay on the following topic:

"Of what value was this Speaking and Imaging Seminar to me?"

Please construct this in the same manner you have constructed your talks. See a Planning sheet for ideas.

•Do not include a discussion of the trainer

•You may include recommendations for future changes in the seminar, if you desire.

•You may share your reactions about the change in a fellow classmate.

•We use this information to improve and up-date the seminar. Thank you!

SPEAKING AND IMAGING FINAL TALK

5-MINUTE TALK ON A POPULAR, APPROPRIATE ISSUE OF YOUR CHOICE

POINT RATING CRITERIA

- 10 points: Planning sheet
- 10 points: Evidence used (3 forms)
- 10 points: Timing--minus 2 for each minute short
- 10 points: Impact on audience
- 10 points: Opening
- 10 points: Closing
- 10 points: Organization of Talk
- 10 points: Animation/enthusiasm
- 20 points: Fulfillment of weekly recommended improvements

PROCEDURE:
- Your name will be called at random.
- You will give your talk.
- Instead of commenting on your talk, your classmates will summarize on back of your card how you have done in course.
- Two minutes will separate talks so class can write.
- No comments will be made by anyone.

THANK YOU FOR YOUR PARTICIPATION!

SECTION TWO

TIPS ON HOW TO BE THE BEST THAT YOU CAN BE

BY GAIL CASSIDY

LIVE THE BEST LIFE YOU CAN
BY BEING THE BEST YOU CAN BE

How can you make your life better than it is now? Hopefully, some of the tips in this booklet will help you live a happier life, especially in your dealings with other people; but first, there are three things you need for yourself. You need food--wholesome and nutritious--to nourish your body. You need shelter--a safe place to live. You need support--someone to let you know you are important to the world.

When you have these three essentials--food, shelter, and support--in your life, you can work on making a difference in the world by positively influencing and impacting the lives of other people. But first, you have to train yourself to FEEL GOOD EVERY DAY. The following chart summaries what is necessary for you to FEEL GOOD EVERY DAY, everyone's ultimate goal.

YOUR PHYSICAL WELL BEING REQUIRES

SOUND NUTRITION AND DAILY EXERCISE

YOUR MENTAL WELL BEING REQUIRES
Always Looking For
Gratitude and Beauty every day
and practicing daily Meditation/Reflection

Everyone's Ultimate Goal is
to feel good!!

To Feel Good, Choose and Experience Any of These
"FEEL GOOD" EMOTIONS:
Passion
Bliss, Happiness
Reverence, Joy
Trust, Optimism
Inspiration
Harmony
Appreciation

Most importantly, every day express GRATITUDE and seek BEAUTY, Validate everyone, look for their positives, and show every one you meet kindness, appreciation, and respect.

THOUGHTS ARE CHOICES and can be either POSITIVE OR NEGATIVE--you make the choice!

TO FEEL BAD, CHOOSE EITHER
JUDGMENT and/or NEGATIVITY
through feelings of
Revenge, Excuses
Procrastination, Anger
Justification, Gossip
Hate, Ill Will, Blame
Sickness, Gloom, Despair
Criticism, Hatred,
Restrictions, Anxiety,
Fear, Shame

THESE FEELINGS EQUAL
DEPRESSION, SADNESS, e.g., "I DON'T FEEL GOOD"

The nice thing is, you have the power and ability to choose to feel good or to feel bad every moment of every day. Choose I FEEL GOOD!

The following tips will help you as you interact with others. Human nature is the same all over the world, and these tips reflect the basics of human relations. Making these tips a part of you will help you be more effective in working with others and will help you maximize your own potential.

Enjoy every day of your life. Each one holds a surprise for you. Look for that surprise each day, and, when you find it, write it down, keep it forever, and see the beauty in whatever occurs.

I wish you all the best in life!!!

Warmly,

Gail Cassidy

GENERAL PHILOSOPHY OF LIVING

1•See the invisible tattoo on everyone's forehead that reads: "PLEASE MAKE ME FEEL IMPORTANT."

2•Find at least one happening in each day to be grateful for.

3•Look for positives in every person.

4•Recognize the specialness of diversity.

5•Provide an atmosphere conducive to happiness, e.g. a smile on your face, comfort, simplicity, etc.

6•Vary your daily activities. Do something different that will revitalize you.

7•Remember, humans of any age need breaks.

8•Know that everyone you meet has something special to offer.

9•Living in the moment is where you find happiness.

10•Learn the Serenity Prayer: "God, grant me the serenity to accept the things I cannot change, courage to change the things I can and the wisdom to know the difference."

11•"See" and/or "feel" your positive day before you climb out of bed. Use positive self talk.

12•Be (or act) enthusiastic about everything you do. It's contagious; it carries over to the people in your life.

13•Accept people as they are, and then provide the atmosphere for them be happy and grow.

14•Learn from every person you meet, every friend.

15•Ask yourself, "Does it really matter?"

16•Being right does not always work, e.g.,

Here lies the body of William Jay, who died maintaining his right of way. He was right, dead right as he sped along, but he's just as dead as if he were wrong.

17•HAVE FUN!

ATTITUDE

18•Park your ego at the door; it hinders relationships with friends and family.

19•Give your friends and people you know a reason to check their negative attitudes at the door also.

20•Know that people "mirror" you. They reflect what they see, hear, and feel from you.

21•Shake things up. Make changes. "If you always do what you have always done, you'll always get what you've always got."

22•Show people through your own example what fun having a great attitude is.

23•Be patient.

24•Positive attitudes are catching, wherever you are.

25•Show respect to get respect.

26•Know that attitude is a choice everyone makes every day.

27•Explain that people cannot help what happens to them, but they are **always** in charge of their responses.

28•Remember, there is a pause between stimulus and response. Choose your response carefully.

29•Ask yourself why you are **choosing** to be unhappy, bored, tired, sad, happy.

30•Know that attitude is the steering mechanism of the brain. Body language can lead to attitude, and vice versa.

31•Practice changing your attitude by sitting or standing straight, with your head up and a smile on your face. It does work!

32•Know that it is the attitude of our hearts and minds that shape who we are, how we live, and how we treat others.

33•Help friends and people you know to recognize their specialness.

34•Success is feeling good about yourself every single day. That is attitude.

35•Know and share with the people you know that true power is knowing that you can control your attitude at all times.

HUMAN RELATIONS

36•Treat everyone as if he or she were your friend's best friend.

37•Never talk down to anyone.

38•Find what is special about every person you meet.

39•**SMILE**. It warms a room.

40•Use tact when responding to a challenging person. The rewards outweigh "being right."

41•Know that it is not okay for people to feel your negativity. That is your choice.

42•Be 100% fair at all times--no exceptions.

43•Keep in mind that perception is reality--yours and your friends' and the people you know.

44•Treat every person as you wish to be treated.

45•Understand that no one **wants** to be wrong.

46•**Everyone desperately wants to feel special.**

47•Remember that people gravitate toward people and things that are pleasurable and avoid people and things that are painful. Make learning pleasurable.

48•LISTENING is the greatest compliment.

49•Try to understand before being understood.

50•Show genuine appreciation to people you interact with.

51•Begin corrective action with sincere and honest recognition of what has been done correctly.

52•Never embarrass anyone. Allow the person to save face.

53•Use encouragement. Make the error seem easy to correct.

54•Don't be afraid to admit your mistakes. It will make you appear more human.

55•Show respect for every person's opinion.

56•Challenge people to be the best that they can be.

57•Make **SINCERITY** your No. 1 priority.

COMMUNICATION

58•Set standards in your everyday life and share them with the people you know.

59•Know the purpose and importance of what you are doing.

60•Set high expectations.

61•Know that 55% of all messages comes from the body. Notice how you can tell your special someone is in a bad mood without any words being spoken.

62•Know that 38% of the message comes from the voice: inflection, intonation, pitch, speed, e.g., "I didn't say he stole the exam." Seven words--seven meanings.

63•Know that you **cannot NOT** communicate.

64•Recognize that we don't all see the same thing when looking at the same thing.

65•Know also that we don't all hear the same things even when listening to the same words.

66•Control your thoughts; your feelings come from your thoughts; therefore, you can also control your feelings! Choice is control.

67•Take responsibility for what you say and how you say it.

68•Listen for the message, yet know that body language can be interpreted as only a clue to the meaning of the message, e.g., arms crossed in front of chest could mean the person is blocking you or could mean the person is actually cold or comfortable.

69•Learn to lead rather than to try and overcome resistance.

70•Communicate your enthusiasm through your body and voice.

71•"One who is too insistent on his own views, find few to agree with him." - Lao-Tze

72•Speak with a warm heart.

SELF-ESTEEM

73•Know that a person with high self esteem does not need to find fault with others.

74•Remember that people find fault with others when they feel threatened, consciously or unconsciously.

75•Know that self-esteem is not noisy conceit. It is a quiet sense of self-respect, a feeling of self-worth. Conceit is whitewash to cover low self-esteem.

76•Remember, people have two basic needs: to know they are **lovable** and **worthwhile**.

77•Remember, it is a person's feeling about being respected or not respected that affects how s/he will behave and perform.

78•Helping people build their self concept is key to being a good friend.

79•Know that your words have power to affect a person's self-esteem.

80•Each person values himself to the degree s/he has been valued.

81•Words are less important in their affect on self-esteem than the judgment(s) that accompany them.

82•The attitude of others toward a person's capacities are more important than his possession of particular traits.

83•Bragging people are asking for positive reflections.

84•Masks are worn to hide the "worthless me."

85•Low self-esteem is tied to impossible demands on the self.

86•A person's own self-acceptance frees him or her to focus on others, unencumbered by inner needs.

87•The single most important ingredient in a nurturing relationship is honesty.

88•Ask this: "If I were to treat my friends as I treat those closest to me, how many friends would I have left?"

89•Avoid mixed messages. Be clear in your statements of expectations.

BOUNDARIES

90•Tolerate no disrespect.

91•Be consistent in enforcing rules.

92•Set boundaries.

93•Find opportunities for others to improve the quality of their work.

94•Differientate between the action and the person.

95•Uncover and address, when possible, the reasons for the person's poor performance.

96•Make sure people you work with have the skills to succeed.

97•Focus, as often as possible, on what is right rather than what is wrong.

98•Give plenty of recognition for the unique gifts of each person.

99•Keep in mind that you have power in the present moment to change your thoughts, feelings, and attitude about the past.

100•Take control of your life by focusing on the present.

101•Remove the word "try" from your vocabulary. "Try" to pick up a pencil. Either you do or you don't.

102•Find the lesson or value in unacceptable situations.

103•Know that you have choices in spite of your past experiences.

104•Turn problems into a learning opportunity.

105•Have a clear vision of where you are going.

106•Approach problematic situations with relaxed confidence.

107•Respond thoughtfully to challenging and/or problem situations.

108•Avoid making judgments.

109•Learn problem solving:
        State the problem
        Look for cause or causes of the problem
        Brainstorm solutions
        Choose the best one

110•Always see beyond your own point of view.

111•Encourage habits of thought conducive to growth in understanding others, to think outside the box.

112•Recognize that there is no one interpretation of a situation.

LIFE'S TREASURE TIPS

113•Begin to be now what you will be hereafter. - St. Jerome. Repetition is the mother of skill.

114•Know that you too are special.

115•Enjoy each day and each moment of life.

116•Make corrections by citing two positives for every negative.

117•Live in the present.

118•Be alert for moments of gratitude.

119•Show lively enthusiasm!

120•Create an atmosphere of fun.

121•Build on successes.

122•Create a routine with varied activities.

123•Turn people on to learning.

124•Visualize doing well.

125•Be relaxed.

126•Make everyone feel important.

127•Remember, "You are what you choose today." -Dyer.

128•Give yourself opportunities to succeed.

129•Provide a safe atmosphere--physically and mentally.

130•Validate yourself frequently.

131•Your reality is what you make it to be.

132•Polish your people skills.

133•Hone your communications skills.

134•Take excellent care of yourself.

MORE TIPS

135•Work towards feeling good about yourself. It is man's highest goal.

136•Always do what you feel is right or true.

137•Your actions reveal your values.

138•Your thought is the most powerful force in your universe. "Nothing is either good or bad but thinking makes it so." -Shakespeare.

139•Be courageous! Whatever you dwell on expands.

140•Work toward goals that cause you to feel a sense of mastery.

141•Write a list of everything you have accomplished or have been recognized for in your life. Add to it whenever you think of something new. Read it when the going gets tough.

142•Have a clear sense of purpose in life.

143•Clarify your goals and focus on them

144•Be a risk taker. Step outside your comfort zone. Try something new.

145•Positive expectations are the single, most outwardly identifiable, characteristics all successful people possess.

146•You can train yourself to think more positively by training yourself to choose what you pay attention to and what you say about it, both to yourself and others. "We know what we are but know not what we may be." -Shakespeare.

147•Whatever you believe, picture in your mind, and think about most of the time, you eventually will bring into reality.

148•Your self-image is the most dominant factor that affects everything you attempt to do.

149•Nothing is more exciting than the realization that you can accomplish anything you really want that is consistent with your unique mix of natural talents and abilities.

150•Remember, "Change your thoughts and you change your world." - Norman Vincent Peale.

WORTHY QUOTES

•Assume a virtue, if you have it not. - Shakespeare.

•Act enthusiastic and you'll be enthusiastic. -Carnegie.

•It is not the place, nor the condition, but the mind alone that can make any one happy or miserable. - L Estrange.

•Beliefs have the power to create and the power to destroy. -Anthony Robbins.

•Nothing is more likely to help a person overcome or endure troubles than the consciousness of having a task in life. -Frankl.

•When the student is ready, the teacher will appear. - Zen proverb.

•The ancestor to every action is a thought. -Emerson.

•Imagination is more important than knowledge. -Albert Einstein.

•Things do not change; we change. -Thoreau.

•Great men are those who see that thoughts rule the world. -Emerson.

•Nothing has any power over me other than that which I give it through my conscious thoughts. -Anthony Robbins.

•The greatest discovery of my generation is that human beings can alter their lives by altering their attitudes of mind.
-William James.

•The only limits you have are the limits you believe. -Wayne Dyer.

•Anything we fail to reinforce will eventually dissipate. -Robbins.

•Patience is the companion of wisdom. -Augustine.

•The more he gives to others, the more he possesses of his own. -Lao-Tze.

•Vision is the art of seeing things invisible. -Swift.

•Believing is seeing. -Dyer.

•We become what we envision. -Claude Bristol

•Change your thoughts and you change your world. -Norman Vincent Peale

•When you discover your life's work, you will realize that you already have the gift to make it happen. -Robert Anthony

•The time to be happy is now. The place to be happy is here, and the way to be happy is by helping others. -Charles Engelhardt

•Finding and creating your life's work will bring you more happiness and money than any other single action you can take. -Robert Anthony

•You make a living by what you get. You make a life by what you give. -Winston Churchill

•Every person I have known who has been truly happy, has learned how to serve others. -Albert Schweitzer

•Life is like a coin. You can spend it any way you wish, but you can only spend it once. -Miguel de Cervantes

•A tragic irony of life is that we so often achieve success . . . after the reason for which we sought it has passed. -Ellen Glasgow

•Give of your hands to serve and your hearts to love. -Mother Teresa

•Until you make peace with who you are, you'll never be content with what you have. -Doris Mortman

•No amount of travel on the wrong road will get you to the right destination.

•Be the change you wish to see in the world. -Mahatma Gandhi

•Our aspirations are our possibilities. -Robert Browning

•What we are seeking is . . . the rapture of being alive. -Joseph Campbell

•I always wanted to be somebody, but I should have been more specific. -Lily Tomlin

•Fear not that thy life shall come to an end, but rather fear that it shall never have a beginning. -John Cardinal Newman

•We do not remember days; we remember moments. -Cesare Pareso

•If the things we believe are different than the things we do, there can be no true happiness. -Dana Telford

•It is only with the heart one can see rightly. What is essential is invisible to the eye. -Antoine de Saint-Exupery

•To be nobody but yourself, in a world which is doing its best to make you everybody else, means to fight the hardest battle which any human being can fight, and never stop fighting. -e.e. cummings

•For this is the journey that men make: to find themselves. If they fail in this, it doesn't matter much what else they find. -James A. Mischner

•I don't know the key to success, but the key to failure is trying to please everybody. -Bill Cosby

•Go confidently in the direction of your dreams. Live the life you've imagined. -Henry David Thoreau

•Destiny is not a matter of chance, but a matter of choice. It is not a thing to be waited for, it is a thing to be achieved. -William Jennings Bryan

•If you are not working on your ideal day, you are working on someone else's. -Marjorie Blanchard

•Experience is not what happens to you. It's what you do with what happens to you. -Aldous Huxley

•When you cease to make a contribution, you begin to die. -Eleanor Roosevelt

•Try not to be a man of success, but a man of value. -Albert Einstein

•The goal is not to have but to be, not to own but to give, not to control but to share, not to subdue but to be in accord . . . not to amass, but to face sacred moments. -Abraham Heschel

•A business that makes nothing but money is a poor kind of business. -Henry Ford

•They may forget what you said, but they will never forget how you made them feel. -Carl Buehner

•Imagine life as a game in which you are juggling five balls--work, family, health, friends, and spirit. Work is a rubber ball. If you drop it, it will bounce back. But the other four balls are made of glass. If you drop one of these, they will never be the same. -Brian Dyson

•There are people who have money and people who are rich. -Coco Chanel

•Success means living the life of the heart. -Frances Ford Coppola

•The work praises the man. -Irish Proverb

•Where the spirit does not work with the hand, there is no art. -Leonardo da Vince

•Opportunities are seldom labeled. -William Feather

•The size of your success is determined by the size of your belief. -Lucius Annaeus Seneca

•It is not hard to make decisions when you know what your values are. -Roy Disney

•Work is love made visible. -Kahil Gibran

•The man who really wants to do something finds a way; the other man finds an excuse. -E.C. McKenzie

•We are what we repeatedly do. Excellence, then, is not an act, but a habit. -Aristotle

•Only those who will risk going too far can possibly find out how far one can go. -T.S. Eliot

•Courage is rightly esteemed the first of human qualities because it is the quality which guarantees all others. -Winston Churchill

•I am a great believer in luck, and I find that the harder I work, the more I have of it. -Thomas Jefferson

•There are no wrong turns, only wrong thinking on the turns our life has taken. -Zen saying

•If we don't change our direction, we are likely to end up where we are headed. -Ancient Chinese Proverb

•Success is getting what you want. Happiness is wanting what you get. -Warren Buffett

•If he was to become himself, he must find a way to assemble the parts of his dreams into one whole. -George Eliot

•Lives based on having are less free than lives based on doing or being. -William James

•The moment that one definitely commits one's self, then Providence moves, too. -Johann Wolfgang von Goethe

•There is no security in life, only opportunity. -Mark Twain

•You miss 100 percent of the shots you never take. -Wayne Gretzky

•All adventures, especially into new territories, are scary. -Sally Ride.

•There is a growing legion of businesspeople who are hungry to build something of enduring character on a set of values they can be proud of. -Jim Collins

•The people who get on in this world are the people who get up and look for

the circumstances they want, and, if they can't find them, make them.
-George Bernard Shaw

•Life shrinks or expands in proportion to one's courage. -Anais Nin

•Don't be afraid to follow your bliss, and doors will open where you didn't know they were going to be. -Joseph Campbell

•If you think you're too small to make a difference, you've never been in bed with a mosquito. -Anita Roddick

•Live neither in the past nor in the future, but let each day's work absorb your entire energies, and satisfy your wildest ambition. - William Osler

•The great use of life is to spend it for something that will outlast it. -William James

===

FAVORITE TOP TEN LISTS
FROM COACH UNIVERSITY COACHES

The Top 10 Ways to Create the Life of Your Dreams

We all deserve to live a happy, fulfilling life. YOU and only you have the power to make that happen. Here are some steps to get you started.

1. **Be quiet!**

Take time to listen to your spirit, your inner voice, whatever you choose to call it. We get too caught up in the day to day stresses and obligations in our lives. Get quiet and tune in to who you really are.

2. **Find a passion.**

Everyone needs to find a passion, but as I stated in number one we are often so over stressed that we don't have a clue to what our passion may be. Here's a start: Take five minutes and write down everything that you love - partners and kids excluded - (we KNOW you love them!)

3. **Find your spirit.**

Life needs to have balance - mind, body and spirit. It's like a three legged stool - with only two legs, or one, it falls over. It doesn't have to be organized religion, it's whatever fills your spirit - a walk on the beach, a hike in the woods, meditation, prayer. Find the force that is bigger than you.

4. **Be grateful.**

I am like a broken record with this - but it's true. Life is always richer when we have appreciation for what we have in our life.

5. Give to others.

Giving of yourself is always a great way to give to yourself. It's a win win situation! Find a cause, a neighbor who's lonely, an animal shelter where they need someone to walk the dogs. It will fill your spirit - just try it!

6. Create intentions and affirmations.

Write down what you want to come in to your life - be specific and positive. Don't use language like "want" - as in "I want a great job." Use a present tense - "I have a job that is fulfilling that I love." It can really work if you say them everyday!

7. Become selfish.

By taking more time to care for yourself you bring more happiness and peace to your life. By loving yourself enough to take care of you, you have more energy and love to give to others.

8. Work on your thoughts.

The most powerful tool you have to change your life is your own thoughts. You can change the way you think to be more loving toward yourself, to be happier, and more at peace. Every time you have a negative thought STOP! and replace it with a positive one.

9. Take time every day to DO something you love.

Make sure you enjoy yourself everyday. Dance, paint, laugh, whatever makes YOU feel wonderful!

10. Get support!

It's not easy to change, it takes determination. Find a friend, hire a coach, get someone who understands what you are trying to do. Life can be a wonderful adventure - it's never too late unless you don't get started!

[Originally submitted by Candace Hammond, Coach University Graduate, Personal and Life Coach, who can be reached at mantis@capecod.net. Copyright 1997, 98, 99, 2000 Coach U]

**The Top 10 Wisdoms to Remember
to Have a Triumphant Life!**

Dear Friend:

To walk triumphantly through life is joyous beyond description, and it can be done! Constructing such a life takes time, and far more wisdom than can be mentioned here. Still, it is hoped you will find this composition to be a refreshing affirmation of some of the core aspects of your life's pilgrimage. Also, may you see that you really are triumphant in so many wonderful ways.

Love to all,
Paul

1. The "Golden Rule"

a. "Do not do unto others all that which is not well for oneself."
Zoroaster, 6th century B.C.E.
b. "Hurt not others with that which pains thyself."
Buddha, 6th century B.C.E.
c. "Do not do unto others what you do not want others to do unto you."
Confucius, 6th century B.C.E.
d. "May I do unto others as I would want that they should do unto me."
Plato, 5th century B.C.E.
e. "Do not do to others which if done to thee would cause thee pain."
Mahabharata, 3rd century B.C.E.
f. "Do not do unto others what thou wouldst not they should do unto thee."
Rabbi Hillel, 1st century B.C.E.
g. "Do unto others as you would have others do unto you."
Jesus, 1st century C.E.
h. "None of you truly have faith if you do not desire for your brother that which you desire for yourself."
Muhammad, 6th century C.E.
i. "Lay not on any soul a load which ye would not wish to be laid upon you and desire not for anyone the things you would not desire for yourself."
Baha'u'llah, 19th century C.E.

2. The "Golden Rule" is not the only rule. The old tried and true axioms are still the best. Review them often and enjoy the trip down memory lane.

Laughter is the best medicine.
It is better to give than to receive.
Two heads are better than one.
Success breeds success.
The mouth speaks what the heart is full of.
An ounce of prevention is worth a pound of cure.
An ounce of pretension is worth a pound of manure.
That which does not kill us makes us stronger.
Time heals all wounds.
Give every crisis two years.
Smile! It increases your face value.

Haste makes waste.
Live life as if you are preparing for the next seven generations.
What's right isn't always popular, and what's popular isn't always right.
Peace is always beautiful.
Wrinkles only show where the smiles have been.
Getting older isn't for wimps.
Have an attitude of gratitude.
Don't count your chickens before they're hatched.
Always drink upstream from the herd.
Question authority. Question reality. Question.
The larger the island of knowledge, the longer the shoreline of wonder.
Ask the right question and the universe will open itself unto you.
Real eyes realize real lies.
Those who dance are thought insane by those who can't hear the music.
Don't take any wooden nickels.
Worry is like interest paid on a debt that never comes due.
You cannot live longer by worrying.
Just direct your feet to the sunny side of the street.
The person who has many friends is truly wealthy.
Hold on tight to your dreams.
Honesty is the best policy.
Unto thine own self be true.
The truth will set you free.

3. **Focus and simplify.**

4. **Know who you are. Celebrate who you are wherever you are. Joyous moments that defy description will happen when you follow your heart. Dreams do come true.**

John Lennon said it best, "There is nowhere you can be that isn't where you're meant to be." Savor every second, even if it means appearing strange to others.

5. **Listen to the Rosa Parks within you.**

No matter how much a person or law may try to tell you what to do and/or deny you of your liberty, do not give up your seat on the bus of life. Don't give up your freedom and integrity. Stand for something or you'll fall for anything. Today's mighty oak is yesterday's nut that held its ground.

6. **We all hit "rock bottom," and sometimes more than once. Learn to get up and start again. If needed, forgive yourself.**

"Don't take life too seriously. You are not going to get out of it alive."

7. **You are not alone!**

8. **According to the late John Denver, "Life ain't nothin' but a funny funny riddle." Have some fun in your life. Here are two riddles:**

a. Make one word out of "NEW DOOR."
b. The poor have it, the rich need it, you'll die if you eat it, it is more evil than the devil, and greater than God. What is it?

Answers appear at the end of the this "Top 10."

9. **Love. Love. Love. You have heard it all before. Here again are some of humanity's statements about love.**

Love is the answer.
Create love.
Make love* not war. (No sexual connotation implied unless you chose to do so.)
Love like there is no tomorrow.
Come on people, now, smile on your brother everybody get together. Try to love one another right now.
Wherever you go, whatever you do, whatever you say, say it with love.
In-A-Gadda-Da-Vida, honey. Don't you know that I love you?
Do what you love and love what you do.
Put a little love in your heart.
Love makes the world go around.
All you need is love.
The greatest is love.
"I love you." The 3 most powerful words. Constantly invent ways to use them.

10. **Have a great life!**

The answer to the first riddle is, "NEW DOOR=ONE WORD."
The answer to the second riddle is, "Nothing." O:-)

[Originally submitted by Paul DuBay, MA, who can be reached at PaulDuBay1@aol.com. Copyright 1997, 98, 99, 2000 Coach U]

The Top 10 Rules for the Game of Life

We have all been given our precious life. How can you take yours to the next level of happiness? Start by realizing the following:

1. **Life is NOT a Game.**

There is no dress rehearsal.

2. **This is YOUR life.**

This is not somebody else's life. Do what you really want to do. Learn to put yourself first.

3. **You no longer have to live by shoulda's, coulda's, oughta's or if only's.**

Live in the present and make each day perfect for you. Have no preoccupations with your past or future. Don't let others' beliefs that don't work for you determine how you will live your life.

4. **There is no such thing as TRYing.**
Simply put, there is really no trying--either you do it or you don't. Put your arms down in front of you; now try to lift your arm. Did you do it? My point is that either you lifted you arm or you didn't. Trying is not full effort and doesn't portray your commitment.

5. **Success is what YOU define it to be.**

If you believe you are successful, you are. Success is measured in numerous ways. If you are intrinsically successful then it would be very difficult not to let

6. **YOU are perfect just the way YOU are.**

Stop focusing on your shortcomings. Start loving yourself and your uniqueness and special gifts.

7. **Listen to YOUR inner wisdom.**

It is this voice or intuition that helps guide you and your decisions.

8. **There are many lessons to be learned.**

There is a lesson to be learned in every triumph as well as every failure. Look for the lessons.

9. **You need to have a vision.**

Having a vision is the first step toward having the life you want. Purpose gives meaning to your life and changes your attitude and perspective about life.

10. **YOU must take actions.**

If you want a more satisfying, fulfilling and balanced life, you must begin taking actions to create it. Status quo is not good enough when you have a gap between where you are and where you want to be. Set goals to support your vision and your dreams. Focus on results and if you're not getting the results you want, find the reason.

[Originally submitted by Natalie A. Gahrmann, M.A., Coach U Graduate, and author, who can

The Top 10 Principles to achieving a life Beyond Balance

Recognition that words like balance or juggling don't fit is finally here! Switching off at work about what is happening at home and putting life into pockets is meaningless. It requires sacrifice or conflict. The beautiful integrated, flowing, harmonious way that people wish to live is beyond this. This Top Ten gives tips for achieving a fulfilled and guilt free life, without sacrificing the people or things you love.

1. **Design the life you want.**

It seems obvious, but it is easier to say what you don't want. Make a clear statement to yourself about the life you want. Be specific. Every day take one step towards achieving that dream - focus on what is possible, not what is impossible. Say no to what you don't want.

2. **Know what your values are.**

Think of a time when you felt honoured, fulfilled, and happy and describe this to yourself or a friend. Listen to how your values show up and from today do nothing that would dishonour these. Ask - what is the cost to me of not honouring my values?

3. **Live your life fully in the moment.**

Be present in every moment, conversation and relationship you have. Know that when you forget this, you lose so much time and energy it is catastrophic. You can waste a day wondering what to do next, instead of enjoying what you are doing. Watch your children - they are experts.

4. **Value your dream time.**

Spend moments just wandering in your head or physically visit the place you dream you will live in or hang out. Gather pictures of what this future will be like. Behave like the person you want to be. Make your dreams real. Now.

5. **Know what your limits are.**

Putting up with things about yourself, the way people treat you, your environment, and your possessions uses up energy that would be better spent else where. Set these limits selfishly!

6. **Chose how you will be.**

I am self-conscious, untalented, unworthy, too busy......No! Say, "Until now I have chosen to be self-conscious, untalented., unworthy, too busy, and from today I chose to be confident, talented, worthy, and live my life at the pace I love"

7. Know what might stop you.

Identify the things that you know might stop you and be ready for them. Identify what you might do to sabotage this process and who might get in your way. Prepare, notice and react positively.

8. Have a support network.

Someone who supports you in your dreams and aspirations and is there for you when you need a friendly face is essential for this to work. A coach, a partner or a friend will keep you on track and encourage you when things get tough.

9. Make now the right time to start.

Listen to yourself say - "This will work when I have more money/time/space/when the kids have grown up…….Give it up! Phrase the things you desire in the here and now

10. Start now.

Have a handful of things that you do every day that are just for you - a good cappuccino, a hot bath, time with your children. This will nurture you and remind you of the commitment you have made to having a beautiful integrated, flowing, harmonious, wonderful, fulfilled life that is YOURS!!

[Originally submitted by Mairi Watson, Founder partner of Professional Life Coaching, Life Coach, who can be reached at mairi@professionallifecoaching.com. Copyright 97, 98, 99, 00, 2001 Coach U]

The Top 10 Steps to a Successful Life

1. Make your intuition your ally.

How does your intuition speak to you? Do you receive information in words, feelings, a body sensation? Do you just know? Ask your intuition questions and pay attention to the answers and act on the information you receive.

2. What are you enthusiastic about?

The root of the word enthusiasm is entheos. It literally means "God Within." Just think, when you feel enthusiastic about your dreams it means that God is speaking through you and saying "yes" to your goals! The feeling of enthusiasm is one of the ways your intuition speaks to you. What makes you excited, happy, delighted? What do you look forward to each day? Do more of it!

3. Be clear about your goals.

We are often quite clear about what we don't want. Spend time thinking about what you do want. What does your ideal life look like? Draw pictures or cut out scenes from magazines that illustrate the life you want to create. Write in your journal, envision. Spend time each day imagining your ideal life. Envision the details of that life. Imagine you are living it now. What are you wearing? What are you feeling? Who are the people around you? The power is within your mind and heart to bring forth the new life you want.

4. Spend time in prayer and meditation.

Answers often come to life's questions through self-reflection. Prayer and meditation are two ways we have of slowing down enough to listen to the still, quiet voice of our Higher Self. Remember that the answers don't always pop into your mind fully formed as you meditate or pray. You may find them slowly evolving into your consciousness over several days or weeks as you ask for insight.

5. Create positive self talk.

Pay attention to what you tell yourself about yourself and your life. If the general tone is hopeful and positive you feel better and are more optimistic. William James said, "The greatest discovery of my generation is that human beings, by changing the inner attitudes of their minds, can change the outer aspects of their lives." It's easier to create a life you love when you give yourself affirmative message.

6. Practice an attitude of gratitude.

Research has shown that the happiest people are the ones who have gratitude for all that they have despite their circumstances. You don't have to postpone happiness until you have achieved all your goals. Joy is an inside job. In the Talmud it says, "In the world to come each of us will be called to account for all the good things God put on this earth which we refused to enjoy." Learn to appreciate the unfolding process of your life, not just the realization of your dreams.

7. Take action.

People often get stuck because they can't figure out how to get from Point A to Point Z. What is one thing you could do that would be a next step? Take a class, talk to a friend, read a book on a topic of interest, learn a new skill. Take action on what feels exciting to you.

8. Look for coincidences and synchronicities.

It has been said that coincidences are God's way of remaining anonymous. We often have serendipity occurring in our lives as a way to show us we are on the right path. As you trust your intuitive knowing you'll find these synchronicities occurring more often.

9. Know that there will be ebbs and flows.

We often reach success through a series of ups and downs. When you are in a "down" place and feeling stuck, know that it won't last forever. Find some ways to enjoy your life despite the lull and continue to focus on what you want.

10. **Trust in divine order.**

Maybe you're beginning to feel as Mother Theresa once did when she said, "I know God will not give me anything I can't handle. I just wish that He didn't trust me so much." The Universe has a perfect plan for your growth and unfolding as a human being. As you learn to be guided by your intuition you're beginning to act on this wisdom from the Universe.

[Originally submitted by Lynn A. Robinson, who can be reached at Lynn@lynnrobinson.com. . Copyright 1997, 98, 99, 2000 Coach U.

The Top 10 Rules for Creating a Better Life

It's said that it's the simple things in life that truly give our lives meaning. Here are 10 tips for creating that better life:

1. **Count your blessings daily.**

Even with life's challenges, there are always positive things, people, and events in our lives that keep us going. Make a list of those things in your life that keep you fueled, and give thanks for them daily.

2. **Do more than you are getting paid to do.**

Going the extra mile brings many unexpected rewards into our life. Remind yourself that it's a privilege to be able to add value to someone else's life.

3. **Shake off your blunders.**

Whenever you get knocked down by life, don't look back on it too long. Mistakes are life's greatest teachers; they help us grow and move on to higher planes, but only if we remain unstuck.

4. **Reward yourself in the best way you can after a period of long labor and achievement.**

Stretch your reward by sharing it with someone special.

5. **Remember that you are God's perfect creation; you can do anything you dream of anytime you want.**

6. **Let your actions always speak of your values.**

Be on guard for false pride and deceit that may halt your progress.

7. **Every day should be unwrapped as a precious gift.**

Life may offer hurdles and stumbling blocks; use these as stepping stones to reaching your goal.

8. Live this day as if it were your last.

Today is all you have. Run with it!

9. Extend everyone you meet all the care, kindness, love, and understanding you can muster, without thought of reward.

Give of yourself: your time, your money, your talent or skills. Take the focus off yourself. Your life will never be the same.

10. Laugh at yourself and at life.

Laughing causes a release of tension and worry, and clears your mind to think clearly toward a solution that is certain to come as soon as you let go.

[Originally submitted by Carmen Stine, Personal Development & Media Coach, who can be reached at coachmentor@aol.com. Copyright 1997, 98, 99, 2000 Coach U]

The Top 10 Ways To Go for It!

When I ask people to list reasons why we hold back and stop short of reaching our goals and living our dreams, the reasons usually involve fear. Fear of failure, fear of success, fear of rejection, fear of not being good enough, fear of looking foolish.

We've all heard that FEAR stands for False Evidence Appearing Real. Here are 10 things you can do to get control of your FEARS and Fully Eliminate All Roadblocks to Success.

1. Listen to your heart.

Norman Vincent Peale wrote that when you have a desire for something that won't go away, that's the voice of God saying that's what you should do. Your heart holds the issues of your life. Listen to it.

2. Dream big.

A client of mine was once driving to Atlanta in her Pugeot. It was a nice car but she wanted a Mercedes, even though she couldn't quite afford it yet. She had a thought accompanied by a strong feeling that "the next time I drive to Atlanta I'll be driving my new Mercedes." Sure enough, that's exactly what happened.

3. Have faith in yourself.

There is no one else on earth like you. Perhaps you want to write a book but don't think it's worth it because so many others have already written a book on your topic. You have a unique perspective that we need to hear. Even an expert can read your book and learn something from you. We're all teachers and we're all students.

4. Have faith in others.

Most people tend to worry too much about what other people think of them. It's your dream; it doesn't matter what others think you should have/be/do. And most people are pulling for you, especially if you're providing a service or product that helps them. They want you to succeed!

5. Have faith in God.

When I started my business, I had many moments of self-doubt and anxiety. How will I get clients? Will I make enough money to survive? One day a thought came to me; it was so strong it almost knocked me over. That thought was, "God got me this far, He won't drop me now." So whenever I have an anxious moment, I think about that, and am able to move forward with courage and faith.

6. Use positive self-talk.

When Moses asked God what His name was, He said, "I Am." What powerful words those are. And whatever adjectives we follow those two words with when describing ourselves will determine who and what we are. If you say, "I am afraid," you'll be afraid. If you say, "I am courageous," you'll be brave. The quality of our lives is determined by our consciousness. ACT successful, and you will be.

7. Visualize positive outcomes.

When pursuing a goal, imagine how success will look to you. What will you have, where will you be, who's with you? All the little details. If you're more kinesthetic than visual, imagine how you'll feel. And if you're more auditory, imagine the sounds of applause and praise you'll receive when you've gotten there and done a good job.

8. Ask, "Is it really too late?"

A woman in her forties wrote to Dear Abby and asked her advice about going to college at her age. It was an unfulfilled dream for her, but she thought she was too old. She said, "I'll be 48 when I graduate." Abby asked her, "And how old will you be then if you don't do it?"

9. Start with a small step.

How do you eat an elephant? One bite at a time. Any task, project, or goal can look almost impossibly huge when you're standing here and looking there. It's enough to make some people give up. You can do it by planning a strategy on how to get there, and writing down the steps with deadlines. When you do it one step at a time, it's much easier.

10. **Hire a coach.**

I probably wouldn't still be in business if it weren't for my coach. Going it alone is hard for even the most dedicated self-starter. A good coach will help you get organized and focused and will guide you to your goal, giving you praise and encouragement along the way. If not a coach, then find a mentor or really good friend who will walk with you all the way. Go For It! You deserve it! If anyone can do it, you can!   [Originally submitted by Annette Estes, Certified Professional Behavioral and Values Analyst, Life Success Coach, who can be reached at aestes@mindspring.com.. Copyright 97, 98, 99, 00, 2001 Coach U]

What the mind can conceive and believe, it can achieve. -Napoleon Hill

HAVE A GREAT LIFE!!!!